Welco.
to

the Ed
Transformation
Nation

— Emma B
Perez

What's the Point of School?

Ed Transformation: A Matter of Life and Death

Emma B. Perez

Dedicated to Ronnie Eliana and Ryker

Contents

Introduction

"The most damaging phrase in the language is 'We've always done it this way!'" - Grace Hopper

Cars have seen many redesigns in the past century; phones are unrecognizable from 100 years ago. Yet, the classroom has not changed since its inception. There is little argument against education reform. No one would say we shouldn't make things better. However, when a system is relatively unchanged for more than a hundred years it can be very hard to "think outside the box." There have been many tweaks within the system over the past decades, but they are not enough. We need to reimagine the structure altogether. For example, let's say the telephone didn't change from a century ago. Then we try to apply the same kinds of tools and software of smartphones to the same piece of hardware as the original. The needs of today do not fit a structure of yesterday. The current design of schools has now become obsolete, and we are far past Education 2.0. Our economies and societies require Education 10 at this point.

In order to make that leap from the original design to what is needed for our children's futures, we first need to establish a new goal. If we keep trying to make reform happen while chasing the same old goal, all we will do is tread water. The new goal I suggest in this book will lead to a culture change that has the power to help us redesign and reprioritize our education system.

This book will explain why a change in structure and culture is quite literally a matter of life and death for our children, and it will offer new ways to think, view, and talk about education. Many of the details of this transformation will be discovered along the way. However, this book will redirect our focus so that we can find a path of true transformation.

Chapter 1: What's the Point?

"Everyone is a genius. But if you judge a fish by its ability to climb

a tree, it will live its whole life believing that it is stupid."

- Attributed to Einstein

What do you think the purpose of school is? Perhaps to prepare children for citizenship, cultivate a skilled workforce, and allow students to compete in a global marketplace? Perhaps to prepare them for college or for life? Now imagine asking a current student what they think the goal is. Would their answer be the same as yours? In my time as a college and career coach I visited high schools all across my state and worked with tens of thousands of students. So, I decided to ask them what they think the purpose of school is. I conducted an online survey and was shocked at what they had to say.[1] Here are just a few of their responses:

I think the goal of the education system is to have the kids pass tests. I feel like no one, not even your parents, really cares if you actually know anything. All they care about is if you passed the test. Passing tests requires more memorization than actual knowledge or mastery of the subject.

The goal of our education system is to standardize not only classes, but students as well. Students are given a superfluous amount of work

---

[1] You can participate in the survey yourself by visiting whatsthepointsurvey.weebly.com

that is supposed to calculate our understanding, crowding our learning with these measures of perfection. Instead of supporting the individuality of each and every student, we lump them into classes and force them to produce what we desire of them. Elective classes are diminishing at an alarming rate, denying a student to express themselves. This, along with developments such as the common core is [stripping] the student's individual understanding of what they are learning.

I believe the current educational system is designed to prepare students for college and standardized tests we take. For example in my calculus class we are not taught what the uses of the equations are. We are simply taught the equations and how to solve problems that appear on the standardized tests and the ACT.

I think the goal of our educational system is to test students, but I think the system is flawed. Our education system is not set up for each type of learner to flourish. The testing system has been unchanged for a long time, and I think testing every single student the same way doesn't show true intelligence. Different types of [learners'] needs should be catered to during adolescence throughout high school. If that was done I think students would have more confidence in themselves and it would also show how smart kids are in different areas.

Nothing but numbers, we are all just numbers with scores and no one cares if those scores benefit us in life or if it has anything to do with anything. It's just a mandatory test, quiz, project, assignment, etc. to tell us whether we meet up to your standards as a society and if we are meant to fit in with the higher, standard or lower education classes.

The goal of our school system is to classify every student by their ability to regurgitate information. We take all these tests, and all these assessments to prove that we are, in their books and definitions, smart, but none of them truly test our intelligence. That's what makes the world go 'round right? Not our ability to remember how to graph a polynomial, but our ability to problem solve and dictate solutions to everyday situations. I remember when I took the ACT: a test that determines my position in the hopes to going to my dream college, and nearly bursting into tears when I was presented with the things I was to be answering. I was overwhelmed with the fact that this is what I was suppose to know...and I didn't know it. I did well for the little amount of time I was given, but the process to getting my scores back was death defying. Our educational system doesn't take into consideration the other possible factors that play a role in our achievements and our daily progress. The only thing they consider is the fact that we are in class with the same title for the subject so we "possibly" all learn the same: incorrect.

At first these responses surprised me because when I was in school I thought the point was to get you into college. However, my time working with high school students led me to realize that the current public school experience is very different from my own, being that they have spent the entirety of their education under the "No Child Left Behind" program. And in the end these responses are on par with the terribly sad experiences and conversations I had with students and teachers on a daily basis. I met a young woman at an affluent school who had lost six friends to suicide. Another young woman, at a not-so-affluent but earnest school, had experienced gun violence in her own home. I met kids that when asked what they wanted to do when they grow up either didn't answer the question, instead saying "well, my parents have already worked it out for me to go to X school to study Y program;" or they genuinely responded with "what do I want to do? Or what am I actually going to do?" I met students who were told they were not "college material" or that they couldn't afford college. At the same time, those students were not shown any alternative. Before their adulthoods had even started they thought they had already lost. I met kids who cried with relief when I assured them that their 3.7 GPA was just fine. I met kids who cried with joy when I showed them education programs for what they wanted to do because they had no idea they even existed. I met so many kids who had already lost hope. Kids who couldn't answer the questions "what do you love to do?" "What are you really good at?" "What do you value?" "What do you want your life to look like?" "What kind of learning environment is best for you?" "How do you make it happen for yourself?"

In trying to find out what had gone wrong — what failed these kids — I decided to start by narrowing down what the goal of school is. What are we trying to accomplish with public, compulsory, paid-for-by-taxation education? So I did some research. As it turns out, it's not about preparing them for life or setting them up for success. I was shocked to find out that the goal is conformity, submission to authority, and university admittance. This may seem like an extreme claim, but a quick trip back in time revealed the truth.

It all began in 18th century Prussia. Johann Gottlieb Fichte, a philosopher who was a key figure in the development and design of public education said,[2]

> *If you want to influence a person you must do more than merely talk to him. You must fashion him. And fashion him in*

[2] Khan, Salman. The One World Schoolhouse: Education Reimagined. New York: Twelve, 2013.

such a way that he simply cannot will otherwise than what you wish him to will.

The idea was not to produce independent thinkers but to turn out loyal citizens who would submit to authority. This was the whole point of public education! One of the tactics they used to help accomplish this was to separate the subjects. Giving each subject approximately an hour, delivering information by lecture, and asking students to attempt application at home away from assistance was specifically designed to prevent independent thinking — to create individuals who submitted to authority — and does not allow for true conceptual learning.

A great analogy for this comes from Sal Kahn:[3]

It was as if they had been taught in two different lessons, how to use a hammer and how to use a screwdriver. Told to hammer, they could hammer. Told to put in a screw, they could use a screwdriver. But told to build a shelf, they'd be paralyzed even though it was just a combination of concepts that they should have learned.[4]

---

[3] Salman Khan is founder of Khan Academy. This online platform provides free lessons, exercises, and videos allowing learners to move at their own pace.

[4] Khan, Salman. The One World Schoolhouse: Education Reimagined. New York: Twelve, 2013.

Initially the system worked because at the time the economy needed lots of worker bees. This was true in the United States as well, so we adopted the system and added to it. In the late 19th century the National Education Association formed the Committee of Ten. This was a group of educators, primarily university presidents, whose mission was to determine what primary and secondary education should be like. They are the ones who decided at what age children would start school, how many years primary and secondary school would be, what children would study, and which subjects were the most important. They felt that each student should get a fair chance to see if they had a capacity for intellectual work. In other words, this is when they began to weed out the manual laborers from the intellectuals.

I agree that each student should get a fair chance to find their unique capacities. However, in that moment a hierarchy was created. To this day, individuals' value is based on their capacity for specific types of academic intelligence. The main problem with this is that people do not come standard, and there is a wide range of intelligences with no one being more important than the others. Over the decades we have created a culture within our schools that creates comparison and causes kids to judge their own individuality. Not only is this profoundly detrimental to the wellbeing of students, this is also the opposite of what is needed for our economy. Companies cannot survive with the same type of person in every position. It is by celebrating our individualities and our unique skills and sensibilities that businesses and economies thrive.

The other topic most discussed in schools other than testing is college. Even in discussions with education reform advocates I still hear the success of a school measured by how many students go to college. But, sending all of our kids to college is detrimental for several reasons. I am by no means suggesting that we should not be encouraging our kids to continue their education after high school. I am suggesting, however, that we should not be sending *all* of our kids *only* to universities. The hierarchy that resulted from the Committee of Ten created a stigma against further education that is not university. The majority of students I spent time with were unaware that there were educational options other than university or community college. Once I pointed out the other options many students would dismiss them because of this focus on university. This stigma has prevented some students from pursuing further education that may have been more suited to their learning styles. It also prevents some students from making fully informed financial decisions when it comes to their higher education. For example, most students today are unaware of apprenticeships. Apprenticeships are education programs that pay students rather than charging them. Every program is different; they may start at $15 an hour or they may pay 50% of full salary. Pay also increases incrementally as you continue in the program. Upon graduation, usually after one to four years, the apprentice will have a job at full salary. My favorite example of this is elevator technician. Full salary for this position averages at $76,000.[5] And this is a profession that is in high demand but in low supply. With this path comes no student debt, job availability, job security, and an active, rather than sedentary, day.

Despite the variety of higher education options, most students who graduate from high school go on to college. This puts an oversupply of individuals into many professions. Because of this oversupply, many recent college grads are having a hard time finding work. In addition, students

---

[5] "How Much Successful Elevator Technicians Make In 2017." OwlGuru.com - Find A Career and College That Suits You. Accessed November 13, 2018. https://www.owlguru.com/career/elevator-installers-and-repairers/salary/.

are going to college in a time of record high tuition costs. Not to mention a degree now takes closer to six years to complete rather than four, thus just adding to the expense.

The stigma against jobs that do not require a university degree prevents most students from considering them. Right now, the majority of tradesmen are retiring. By 2025 there will be approximately one million jobs left vacant and that number will only grow.[6] This is concerning considering the fact that these jobs are integral to our livelihoods. According to the Bureau of Labor Statistics, some of the professions with the most new jobs includes laborers and home health aids, among others.[7] These require an education that is not as expensive or time consuming as a university degree. Rejecting these types of careers as an option is so automatic and pervasive that when I asked what makes it such a bad choice, many students couldn't answer why. With these industries being so important and the fact that they can offer competitive wages, they should not be dismissed so easily, but we shouldn't stop there. Our schools teach

---

[6] Valet, Vicky. "10 High-Paying Blue-Collar Jobs 2018." Forbes. June 25, 2018. Accessed August 15, 2018. https://www.forbes.com/sites/vickyvalet/2018/06/25/10-high-paying-blue-collar-jobs-2018/#2f4778403311.

[7] "Most New Jobs : Occupational Outlook Handbook:." U.S. Bureau of Labor Statistics. April 13, 2018. Accessed August 15, 2018. https://www.bls.gov/ooh/most-new-jobs.htm.

kids that if they do what is expected of them and go to college they will get a job. That simply does not cut it anymore. A college degree used to essentially guarantee a job. That is no longer the case. Many people now create their career paths. Job sharing, freelancing, consulting, and multiple streams of income are all things that are extremely important to understand today.[8] Employers are looking for creative, innovative thinkers who work well both individually and in teams. Furthermore, many students in primary and secondary school today will go on to have jobs that don't even exist yet. It is not about simply getting a job anymore.[9] It's about creating a career path, a lifestyle, a niche of one's own particular expertise.

Sending all of our students to college is not only an economically poor choice; it is sometimes a poor choice for the individual. I say sometimes because for many individuals, college is the right path. However, there are also many students in college even though it is not the right path for them. According to the National Center for Education Statistics barely over half

---

[8] Nearly 50% of adults under the age of 40 are freelancers. It is no surprise then that a study has predicted freelancers to become the U.S. workforce majority within the next decade.

[9] "Freelancers Predicted to Become the U.S. Workforce Majority within a Decade, with Nearly 50% of Millennial Workers Already Freelancing, Annual "Freelancing in America" Study Finds I Press, News & Media Coverage." Hiring I Upwork. October 28, 2017. Accessed August 15, 2018. https://www.upwork.com/press/2017/10/17/freelancing-in-america-2017/.

of those who enter college finish.[10] Often, it is because college is not the right type of environment for these learners. Even many of those who do finish and who manage to find a job discover that they are not happy in those roles. After following all of the rules, doing what they were supposed to do, and getting a job that pays them comfortably, they expect to be happy. However, some find that this is not the case. I read a story of a woman who followed the rules and got lucky enough to have a good office job that paid well, but she quickly burned out and decided to leave it all behind. Instead she found her happiness living on an island with low cost of living and working at an ice cream shop. It may not sound like "the dream" to some of us, but for her it was perfect. Her needs were met and she had more time to enjoy her life. The response to her story was admiration for being so brave. Now imagine that she, upon graduating from high school, knew that the path she was expected to take would make her unhappy, so instead she decides at 18 years old to move to an island to work at the ice cream shop. Would she have been met with the same admiration? Probably not. Yet she would have avoided years of stress

---

[10] "The NCES Fast Facts Tool Provides Quick Answers to Many Education Questions (National Center for Education Statistics)." Revenues and Expenditures for Public Elementary and Secondary Education: School Year 2001-2002, E.D. Tab. Accessed August 15, 2018. https://nces.ed.gov/fastfacts/display.asp?id=40.

and unhappiness which can both lead to poor health.

There are many people who thrive climbing the corporate ladder and many who despise it. However, most students in today's education system will not be guided to finding out what jobs and lifestyles suit them best, and they most certainly are not guided on how to create a life for themselves based on their interests. They are left, just as we were, to "find themselves," on their own, after graduating from high school and entering the workforce.

The hierarchy created by the Committee of Ten also stigmatizes certain subjects. This created an education system that teaches only to certain types of intelligences, not all. As Sir Ken Robinson puts it, "the question shouldn't be 'how intelligent are you.' It should be 'how are you intelligent.'"[11] Not only are we telling students that they should not be exploring certain intelligences or careers, we are also telling them that there are only a few that are suitable. This stigma and suppression of certain types of skills and talents is not only creating an unbalanced

[11] Robinson, Ken, Sir. "Do Schools Kill Creativity? I Sir Ken Robinson." YouTube. January 06, 2007. Accessed August 15, 2018. https://www.youtube.com/watch?v=iG9CE55wbtY.
Sir Ken Robinson is an author, speaker, and global leader in reimagining education. His "Do Schools Kill Creativity?" is the most watched TED Talk of all time. He works with governments, education systems, international agencies, global corporations and some of the world's leading cultural organizations.

economy and leaving our education in an antiquated system, but it also creates many unhappy individuals believing that they are stupid and/or inadequate.

In preparing students for a future we cannot predict, it is best to give students everything they need to be happy, healthy individuals who know: how to manage their lives; what their strengths, interests, and values are; and how to turn those into a financially sound career. Our current education system is not set up to do that. It is time that the focus of our schools shift to the individual student. The success of a school should not be measured by how many of their graduates are admitted to college. It is more important that individuals be able to manage their inner world, relate to their outer world, and find their place in the world. We need individuals to know themselves, know their communities, and know how to create a comfortable and happy life based on their interests and skills.

Chapter 2: Preparing for an Economy and a Society that Doesn't Exist Yet

"Craft the life you want. Leave the world better than you found it."

- unknown

At the beginning of this century we had no idea what social media marketing was or how important a role it would end up playing, yet just 10 short years later it became essential. This is just one example of how quickly the workforce changes and in ways that are unpredictable. To find a new goal for our education system, it is a good idea to try to determine what our children need to be prepared for. But, that would require predicting the future. How do we then prepare kids for jobs and lives in a future that we cannot predict? In contemplating this question there are a few things one would need to consider.

First, we are going to look at the trends. While signs will point in a direction, there really is no way of knowing which way things will go for sure, but it is still an exercise worth tackling. Next, we are going to redefine the word "success." Success for current and future generations is not the same as it was for previous generations. Finally, we will talk about a different direction for education that could adequately prepare kids for the economy and society of the future.

The Trend

We are at the beginning of a Digital Industrial Revolution. It is a historical shift much like the Industrial Revolution of two hundred years ago. However, this Digital Industrial Revolution is changing much more quickly than the revolution of the last millennium. Marco Annunciate is Chief Economist at General Electric. A large part of his job is to predict the jobs of the future. He explains,

> A *plausible horizon for these new technologies to really spread and transform the industrial system and the economy as we know it, you're thinking a horizon of 20-25 years. But that's for the complete transformation. Within the next 5-10 years we will already see very substantial changes. I'm saying this because some of these changes are already taking place.*[12]

Maurice Conti is Head of Applied Research and Innovation at 3D design and engineering software company, Autodesk. He tells us that humans will work with technology, a partnership he is calling "augmentation" rather than "improvement." "If we work with technology we will improve outcomes even more than either of us can do on our own."[13] He argues

---

[12] Raz, Guy. "The Digital Industrial Revolution." NPR. Accessed August 15, 2018. https://www.npr.org/programs/ted-radio-hour/522858434/the-digital-industrial-revolution.

[13] "The Digital Industrial Revolution." Interview by Guy Raz. Https://www.npr.org/programs/ted-radio-hour/522858434/the-digital-industrial-revolution. Ted Radio Hour. April 21, 2017.

that in some cases professions will be replaced, but in most cases that is not true. With every new piece of technology there are new opportunities. While some technologies may replace jobs that exist now, they will create new opportunities, new jobs. Human/technology collaboration is better than either one working on their own. "It's a little bit like a dance. The human might lead, but the computer can do lots of fancy moves that together combine into something that is greater than the sum of its parts."

Jack Ma is the founder and executive chairman of Alibaba Group, a conglomerate of internet-based technology and artificial intelligence businesses. He is known globally as a leading innovation visionary. He explains,

> *Education is a big challenge now. If we do not change, 30 years later we'll be in trouble. The way we teach, the things we teach, are the things of the past 200 years. It's knowledge based. We cannot teach our kids to compete with machines. We have to teach them something unique. Values, believing, independent thinking, teamwork, care for others... knowledge will not teach you that. We should teach our kids sports, music, art, making*

sure humans are different from machines.[14]

Ma is right. We cannot continue to educate for the economy of the previous centuries. Our economy is going through a massive shift, so our education has to change to meet its needs.

Redefining Success

Merriam-Webster tells us success is a favorable or desired outcome. However, our culture has defined success in a more nuanced way. You might have heard this one: "Go to college and get a job." This suggests that if you go to college you will end up with a well paying white collar job that will provide financial freedom. You might have also heard this one: "Follow your dreams and pursue your passions." This suggests that those seeking only financial success are living unfulfilled lives; only in finding the job of your passions will you be happy. Our current culture teaches that what you do for a living is the main measure of success. Whether what you do brings you money or passion, it tends to be our professions that defines us.

However, we cannot continue to put all of our eggs in one basket like

---

[14] WorldEconomicForum. "Jack Ma: "If We Do Not Change the Way We Teach, Thirty Years from Now We Will Be in Trouble."" YouTube. January 24, 2018. Accessed August 15, 2018. https://www.youtube.com/watch?v=pQCF3PtAaSg.

this anymore. A college degree does not always bring the financial freedom that it once did in generations past. Having a single stream of income is dangerous in our current economy. Tying our identities to our professions can be emotionally detrimental. For some, putting the burden of sustaining our lives onto our passion can end up killing that passion. Those who make a sustainable living from their passion have hit the jackpot. The rest of us should no longer be seen as unsuccessful. What we do for income is only a piece of the puzzle that is our life. It needs to fit, yes, but it is not the only thing that defines us.

Success should no longer be about what you do for a living, but about achieving a personal standard of excellence. It should be about setting goals for ourselves and developing character traits to help us persist in our goals. This type of study needs to be made a priority in schools. For example, a character trait which we must emphasize in schools is grit. Studies have shown that grit is a significant predictor of success. Angela Duckworth has conducted studies across many areas to find what determines success.[15] She found that it was not IQ scores or the ability to

---

[15] Duckworth, Angela. "Success." Interview. Https://www.npr.org/2013/10/25/240777690/success. Ted Radio Hour. November 1, 2013.

learn quickly and easily that lead to success in school and life. Grit emerged as the most significant predictor of success. So, what is grit? Duckworth tells us it is simply stick-to-it-iveness. It's about stamina; the ability to stick with things even when they get challenging. Grit is a byproduct of a growth mindset. Growth mindset is the belief that the ability to learn is not fixed. It can change based on your effort.

We need to help young people find what their definition of success is for themselves. Help them design a life, determine what careers, or jobs, or income streams will fit within that design, plan for contingencies, and then help them find the further education they need to achieve their personal success. College and career exploration should be about designing a life, not just getting a job.

Job Preparation

Putting all of this together, we see that due to the digital industrial revolution, jobs are changing quickly. We cannot afford not to change with them. We need to instill skills and character traits that allow for adaptability. We are moving into a future of waning resources, growing populations, climate change, and quickly changing technology. We need to differentiate ourselves from machines, we need to give our kids the skills to solve large-scale problems, and we need to change our thinking from merely job preparation to life design. This requires teaching students how to solidify their values and their belief systems. We need to teach kids to be altruistic, to be independent thinkers, to be globally minded, and to be solution-oriented problem solvers. We need to give them the knowledge to care for their physical, emotional, and financial well-being. This is what will lead to adaptability and success in the workplace and in all areas of their lives.

Chapter 3: The Five Happy Healthy Elements

"We can't become what we need to be by remaining what we are."

- Oprah

The economy has changed and people's needs have changed. It is far past time that we change the reason why we go to school. Rather than testing, standardization, and college attendance, the goal should be to help our kids live happy, healthy lives. As our society's stress levels increase, weight increases, and chronic illness diagnoses increase, the life expectancy for kids today has declined relative to their parents.[16] This is the first time this has occurred in centuries. It is far past time that we give more priority to ensuring that our schools teach kids to live happy, healthy lives. Based on my studies, I believe this can be accomplished by incorporating five key focus areas that I call the Five Happy Healthy Elements (5HHE).

The Five Happy Healthy Elements (5HHE):

- Emotional Health & Positive Relationships
- Physical Health & Nutrition
- Financial Literacy
- Community Involvement & Effective Altruism
- Play & Exploration of Interests

[16] Fredrickson, Barbara. "Love 2.0: How Our Supreme Emotion Affects Everything We Think, Do, Feel, and Become." New York: Hudson Street Press, 2013.

As I have been developing the Five Happy Healthy Elements, I have noticed that people tend to dismiss the word "happy." I think this is due to the fact that some think of happiness as an intangible state or a subjective feeling. The good news is that happiness is in fact both teachable and measurable. Dr. Ed Diener, also known as Dr. Happiness, tells us that a self-reported measure of happiness is actually the best. This measure will match to:

- Brain scans of the left prefrontal activity

- Serotonin and cortisol levels

- What family and friends say about one's happiness level

- Reaction time to good and bad things

- Memory for good vs. bad.

He was also able to predict future behavior based on happiness levels. People who are more cheerful and satisfied at 18 years old later succeed in life in certain ways. They tend to have higher incomes, are more likely to live longer, have better health, and are more likely to get married and stay married.[17]

For the country of Bhutan, measuring GNH, or Gross National Happiness,

levels is a matter of national pride.[18] The Bhutanese state,

> *GNH is a much richer objective than GDP or economic growth. In*
> *GNH, material well-being is important but it is also important to*
> *enjoy sufficient well-being in things like community, culture,*
> *governance, knowledge and wisdom, health, spirituality and*
> *psychological welfare, a balanced use of time, and harmony with*
> *the environment.[19]*

They regularly survey the citizens to measure happiness. The Director of

the Centre for Bhutan Studies and GNH Research said: "The GNH Index

provides a self-portrait of a society in flux, and offers Bhutanese the

opportunity to reflect on the directions society is moving, and make wise

and determined adjustments." Because of this focus they are able to say:

---

[17] Diener, Ed. "Pursuit of Happiness." Pursuit of Happiness. Accessed August 15, 2018. http://www.pursuit-of-happiness.org/history-of-happiness/ed-diener/.
Ed Diencer is professor of psychology at the University of Utah and the University of Virginia and is one of the leading pioneers in scientific research on happiness for the past twenty-five years. His Satisfaction with Life Scale is one of the many protocols he developed that is used widely in positive psychology, the scientific study of what makes life worthwhile. He is chiefly responsible for coining and conceptualizing the aspect of happiness which can be empirically measured—"Subjective Well Being" (SWB).

[18] Bhutan is a small country on the Himalayas' eastern edge with landscapes that range from subtropical plains to steep mountains and valleys.

[19] Grossnationalhappiness.com. Accessed August 15, 2018. http://www.grossnationalhappiness.com/.

91.2% of Bhutanese are narrowly, extensively, or deeply happy and 43.4% of Bhutanese are extensively or deeply happy.

In addition to being measurable, happiness is also teachable. There are a few places to learn about the pursuit of happiness. Dr. Roger Walsh[20] has been researching how to enhance wellbeing — physical, psychological, social and spiritual for over 30 years. His research has lead to the 8 Ways of Wellbeing project.[21]

These 8 ways include:

Nutrition	Spirituality
Exercise	Time in Nature
Relationships	Recreation
Giving Back	Relaxation

For something more structured, you can take a class that teaches how to live a life of happiness and fulfillment. Dr. Rajagopal Raghunathan, speaker and professor at the Indian School of Business, answers the question "If you're so smart, why aren't you happy?" His course is now

---

[20] Dr. Walsh is professor of Psychiatry, Philosophy and Anthropology at the University of California, Irvine.

[21] Walsh, Roger, Dr. 8 Ways to Wellbeing. Accessed August 15, 2018. https://www.8waystowellbeing.com/.

accessible to anyone on Coursera.[22] Dr. Raj, as he likes to be called, explains that happiness is like a balloon. He talks about specific ways in which we tend to poke holes in our balloons, thus deflating our happiness. He also teaches seven habits of the highly happy to help us "inflate the balloon." To increase happiness, we need to patch the holes. The more of the seven happy habits we use, the more our balloons will inflate.[23] As with any habit, these happy habits need to be practiced.

Because happiness does require practice that is all the more reason to incorporate it into schooling. Children have different learning styles and varied interests. This is why personalized learning plans are starting to grow. However, there are a few things that are universally fundamental such as literacy and numeracy. Everyone needs to know how to read and calculate. I believe we need to add the Five Happy Healthy Elements to this list of fundamentals. I began to contemplate what it could look like if we changed the goal of our education system to make happiness a priority and to make the 5HHE fundamental. I discovered that it is in redirecting

---

[22] Coursera is an organization that partners with top universities around the world to provide access to their online courses for free. coursera.com

[23] Raghunathan, Rajagopal, Dr. "A Life of Happiness and Fulfillment." Coursera. Accessed August 15, 2018. https://www.coursera.org/learn/happiness.

our focus to teaching kids how to thrive that we can start to see a new path for education. Let's look in more detail at what the new goal for education should be and what it will look like if we pursue it.

The New Goal

In Sir Ken Robinson's book, *Creative Schools*, he points out that we should and could be helping students to manage their inner world and relate to their outer world.[24] I would take that one step further and add that we can also help them to find their place in the world. But what does all of that mean?

Help students to manage their inner world:

- knowing themselves well
- managing their emotions
- recognizing positive vs. negative relationships
- managing their physical health

---

[24] Robinson, Ken, and Lou Aronica. "Creative Schools." UK: Penguin Books, 2016.

Help students relate to their outer world:

- having a positive money mindset

- making informed decisions about their finances

- expanding their world beyond their immediate circle

- taking positive action in their communities

Help students to find their place in the world:

- give them the time and resources to play and explore interests

- learn their values and unique skills

- learn how to turn their interests, skills, and values into a career

- learn what steps they need to take and what kind of further education they need to get to that career

It was with this prompt from Sir Robinson along with the other happiness studies that I formulated the Five Happy Healthy Elements. By making these elements a priority in addition to restructuring the classroom through various methods including teaching through interests, emphasizing growth mindset, and shifting the role of the educator, we will make the greatest impact on the lives of young people. If we can accomplish this new transformation then we will decrease violence, depression, anxiety, substance abuse, and the number of incarcerated individuals. And we will create a more positive society by increasing understanding and kindness, participation in civil duties, and economic growth. In order to show how these five elements can make that kind impact, let's take a closer look at each in turn.

Chapter 4: Play and Exploration of Interests

"If we don't stand up for children then we don't stand for much."

- Marian Wright Edelman

Play

The first Happy Healthy Element we will focus on is one that is hugely important for a child's development in many areas. No only does it helps children manage their inner world *and* relate to their outer world, it is the Happy Healthy Element that most directly helps children find their place in their world.

Dr. Peter Gray is an evolutionary biologist who studies play in mammals.[25] He explains that young mammals of all species play. Play allows them to build their bodies, establish various life and social skills, and take risks in safe environments. He also points out that the larger the mammal's brain, the more play it needs for proper development. Researchers have conducted experiments that deprive young mammals of the opportunity to play while they are growing up. The result is that when they grow up they are socially and emotionally crippled. Play is hugely essential to the proper development of mammals' bodies and minds.

Despite all of this, it has been documented that over the last 60 years

[25] Dr. Peter Gray is a Research Professor of Psychology at Boston College. He is also author of "Free to Learn: Why Unleashing the Instinct to Play Will Make Our Children Happier, More Self-Reliant, and Better Students for Life."

free play has been slowly taken away from children.[26] In the 1950s, for example, the school year was five weeks shorter than it is today. The school day was six hours long, but in elementary school, two of those hours were spent outside playing. This included a 30-minute recess in the morning, a 30-minute recess in the afternoon, and a full hour for lunch during which students could go to the playground if they liked. They were never in a classroom for more than an hour at a time. Homework was only for high school students and they had much less than students do now. While outside of school they had chores or even part time jobs they also had plenty of time for free play. Dr. Gray points out that he is talking specifically about free play, self-controlled and self-directed.

Over the same decades that play has declined we have also seen a well-documented increase in all kinds of mental disorders in children. Gray tells us that five to eight times as many children today suffer from major depression or a clinically significant anxiety disorder. We have seen a doubling of the suicide rate among young people ages 15-24. We have seen a quadrupling of the suicide rate in children ages 15 and under. We

---

[26] Gray, Peter, Dr. "The Decline of Play." YouTube. June 13, 2014. Accessed August 15, 2018. https://www.youtube.com/watch?v=Bg-GEzM7iTk.

have also seen a continuous decline in children's sense of control over their lives. They believe their lives are controlled by fate, circumstance, and by other people's decisions. In more recent years we have seen a decline in empathy and a decline in creative thinking.

Dr. Gray is careful to point out that it is true that correlation does not prove causation. However, he shows that the correlation in this case is particularly good. The increase in anxiety and depression has not correlated with economic cycles or war. As a matter of fact, children today are more depressed than they were during the Great Depression and more anxious today than during the Cold War. In addition, these are the effects that are expected when free play is taken away. Free play is where we have control over our lives, where we learn to solve problems, where we experience joy, and where we practice empathy.

In addition to all of these conclusions, Dr. Gray makes some wonderful suggestions as well. He advises having supervisors at parks, creating adventure playgrounds like the ones you see in Europe, opening up school gymnasiums after school for free play, and blocking off streets at certain times for play. He encourages people to get to know their neighbors and he calls for action in our education system: "we need to stand up against the clamor for more school. Our children don't need more school. Maybe they need better school but they don't need more school."

While free play is important for children's development, even game play has benefits for children and adults for many reasons:[27]

- Parents who spend more time playing with their kids have better relationships with them.

- Play allows us to stay connected with those in our social network.

- Play can outperform pharmaceuticals for treating clinical anxiety and depression. Just 30 minutes of gameplay, including video games, is enough to create dramatic boosts in mood and long-term happiness.

- Play leads to exploration of self and interests. Exploring interests helps us find our passions.

Exploration of Interests

Not only is play absolutely essential for proper development, it is also the foundation of career exploration. In addition to allowing ample time for play, our schools need to be spending more time on career exploration

[27] McGonigal, Jane. "The Game That Can Give You 10 Extra Years of Life." TED: Ideas worth Spreading. Accessed August 15, 2018. https://www.ted.com/talks/jane_mcgonigal_the_game_that_can_give_you_10_extra_years_of_life.

with middle school and high school students.

All of us look for what some people call our purpose. Others call it life direction, or career path. Regardless of what you call it, here in the United States we have an innate desire to follow the "American Dream." In order to discover what our path is, we need to discover a few essential things: our values, our skills, and our interests.

It is through play that we discover what our interests are. Our interests are what helps us find the industries we would be happiest pursuing. Play also helps us learn what our innate skills are, which skills we can improve upon, and which skills to outsource. It is our skills that help us identify the specific jobs within an industry that would suit us best. Also, when we know what our skills and talents are we can have confidence in what we bring to the work we do. By knowing our values, we are able to make decisions in order to stay true to ourselves and possibly even to find work that allows us to be part of something bigger. It is in the combination of these three that we will find our purpose, our passion, or our life direction.

Interests –> Industry   Values –> Decision   Skills –> Job

Interest + Skill + Values = Purpose

In my time as a college and career coach for high school students I discovered that most students could not even define the world value much less tell you what their values are. Some students, but not all, may have an understanding of what some of their skills are. And for some students an interest may be explored, but depending on what it is, they will receive more or less time to explore this interest. And only for some are these interests explained in terms of industry or career path. I worked with some amazing teachers who wanted to make sure that their students received access to these self-discovery opportunities. But often I was the only one bringing these exercises to them, and even then they only had it for one day. We need to be making career exploration, job shadowing, and internships a much higher priority for our older students.

Play has an extremely important role in all areas of a child's life. It should be prioritized and it should evolve as children grow. For younger students we need to facilitate the time and environment to allow free play. The Waldorf education model is one example of this.[28] Play is prioritized and an emphasis is placed on arts and crafts, music and movement, and

---

[28] "Home - Association of Waldorf Schools of North America." Waldorf Education - Association of Waldorf Schools of North America. Accessed December 12, 2018. https://www.waldorfeducation.org/.

nature.

As students grow older they should begin to explore and dig more deeply into their interests. Middle school is a good time to begin job shadowing with the ability to explore many different options. Once they reach the teen years the focus should shift to how to find or create a career path based on their individual talents, skills, values, and interests. Finally, we need to give them adequate guidance to find the kind of further training or schooling they need to achieve their careers. It is in guiding students gradually and from an early age in this kind of self-discovery that they they will be better able to, at 18, answer the question "What do you want to do?"

Chapter 5: Emotional Health and Positive Relationships

"Educating the mind without educating the heart is no education at all."

- Attributed to Aristotle

Emotional Health

This Happy Healthy Element is all about helping children manage their inner worlds and relate to their immediate circles. Emotional health training is sorely lacking in society in general. Regardless of one's socioeconomic status, religious background, or home life most of us are not taught how to manage our emotions. Developing the skills required to regulate your emotions and take control of your feelings is not easy. And, like other skills, this requires time and practice.

What exactly is emotional health? It is about learning how to regulate feelings and the thoughts that lead to those feelings. When you are able to control your emotions your prefrontal cortex is more available for you to make good decisions.[29] Many studies have shown that having this kind of self control correlates with:

- Better adjustment (fewer reports of psychopathology, higher self-esteem)

- Less binge eating and alcohol abuse

- Better relationships and interpersonal skills

---

[29] Tangney, June P., Roy F. Baumeister, and Angie Luzio Boone. "High Self-Control Predicts Good Adjustment, Less Pathology, Better Grades, and Interpersonal Success." Journal of Personality 72, no. 2 (2004): 271-324. doi:10.1111/j.0022-3506.2004.00263.x.

- Secure attachment

- Better grade point average

- More optimal emotional responses

Because of this, social and emotional learning is starting to gain traction in schools, but it is still rare to see and is often up to individual teachers to decide to and take the time to incorporate this kind of learning. These skills will positively influence a child immediately and throughout their lives. Understanding and managing emotions is the foundation that is needed to relate to others in all kinds of situations. It is the groundwork for positive relationships, whether they be familial, friendly, or professional.

Positive Relationships

Teaching children how to have positive relationships not only encourages positivity, builds confidence, and teaches good manners, but also helps children identify harmful relationships. Physical harm is much easier to spot than is emotional harm. Most people in general minimize the impact that negative individuals and relationships can have in our lives.

Our schools could help children to be a positive force in their relationships, teach them how to spot negative relationships and what to do when they come across them.

One of the many concerns I learned about when working with schools was how much a student's home life impacts their educational life. And of course it does. I'm sure you have had situations where something stressful was happening at home and you found it harder to compartmentalize and keep focused at work. How can a kid focus in class when they are hungry, or their dad has berated them because they didn't get the grades he demands, or they are worried about where their mom is? Ask any teacher and they can tell you multiple stories about being able to tell when a kid has had something negative happen at home because of the obvious changes they exhibit at school.

Parent participation is a focus in all schools because of the overwhelming evidence that children perform better academically if they have parents involved in their children's learning, but this is a double-edged sword. On one end of the spectrum, we have kids who do not have an adult advocating for their education. On the other end, we have kids pushed too hard leading to exhausted, externally driven, impaired children who believe that they are "only as good as their last performance."[30]

Safe Haven

Unfortunately, far too many children have a variety of things that greatly impact their lives in negative ways. Not only do our schools not help kids cope with these things, the way our school systems is designed and prioritized often contributes to the stress and emotional distress that children face. Why shouldn't our schools be a safe haven for kids? Why not make it a priority to give kids communities of peers and adults to help them manage their struggles? Why not teach them skills they can use throughout their lives to handle negative situations?

I was so excited to find a few amazing examples of how this is accomplished. Urban Prep in Chicago has prioritized a class called Pride Advisory.[31] This class is focused on building character and supporting social and emotional needs. In freshman year, kids are placed in a group of peers with an adult Pride Leader who has a background in social work.

---

[30] Levine, Madeline. Teach Your Children Well: Parenting for Authentic Success. New York: Harper Perennial, 2013.

[31] Edutopia. "Pride Advisory Classes: Social and Emotional Support for Every Student." YouTube. March 18, 2016. Accessed August 15, 2018. https://www.youtube.com/watch?v=6BACoWFiRzE.

This group will remain the same throughout their high school experience allowing for bonds to form with their peers and an adult at their school. In this class, which as you can imagine becomes a second family, they are given skills to better navigate their lives in and out of school. They have a framework full of wide ranging topics, including safe sex practices, stress management, and concerns that the kids want to discuss. And the kids soak it up! They are hungry for it. I noticed even in my little bits of advising that kids were so grateful for the attention and positive, supportive guidance I gave them. As for Urban Prep, they have an attendance rate of 94%, higher than the national average.

The Holistic Life Foundation, a nonprofit in Baltimore, recently started aiding schools in creating an "Oasis of Calm" room that replaces detention.[32] Here, not only do students work with behavioral professionals, but they also practice mindfulness techniques. The results are amazing. Two years after the program began, not one suspension has been issued.

Mindfulness

Mindfulness is the therapeutic technique by which we learn how to

[32] "EMPOWERING COMMUNITIES." Holistic Me After School Program I Holistic Life Foundation. Accessed August 15, 2018. https://hlfinc.org/.

manage our emotions. While mindfulness has its roots in meditation, often associated with eastern religions, this secular practice has entered the American mainstream in recent years. It is about learning to observe your thoughts and feelings in a third person way, separating from them so that you can access them and make choices without judgement. Through mindfulness practice, we learn to assess our surrounding environment, emotions, bodily sensations, thoughts, and feelings.

Since the late 1970s, mindfulness techniques have been used in countless programs in hospitals, prisons, veterans centers, and more. Thousands of studies have documented that practicing mindfulness, even for a few weeks, can have a variety of physical, psychological, and social benefits including: boosting our immune systems; increasing positive emotions while reducing negative emotions and stress; and serving as an effective antidepressant.[33] Mindfulness also improves attention skills. It boosts altruism and self-compassion as well as enhances relationships. Mindfulness can even fight obesity through "mindful eating." Meditation and mindfulness literally changes the brain by increasing the gray matter

---

[33] Marchant, Jo. "Future - Can Meditation Help Prevent the Effects of Aging?" BBC News. July 01, 2014. Accessed August 15, 2018. http://www.bbc.com/future/story/20140701-can-meditation-delay-ageing.

in brain regions linked to learning, memory, emotional regulation, and empathy, and can prevent or slow aging on a cellular level.[34]

I remember when I first shared the Oasis of Calm program on social media I was met with "well, then the kids will do anything they can to be there instead of in the classroom." This suggests a fear that classroom management will be worse if this option is made available. However, I pointed out that instead, we should focus on the *why* behind kids preferring the Oasis of Calm. It's because that kind of emotional support is sorely needed. Fortunately, there are ways to incorporate bits of stress management and mindfulness into the classroom regardless of what you teach. This is extra education that teachers often have to seek out for themselves in their own time and at their own expense which is a lot for them to do on top of all of their requirements and regulations. This is why I advocate to make it a priority in all schools, allowing time and funds to go towards this kind of application.

Helping students manage their emotions will, of course, help with classroom management and instill employability skills, but more

---

[34] Lazar, Sara, Dr. "How Meditation Can Reshape Our Brains." YouTube. January 23, 2012. Accessed August 15, 2018. https://www.youtube.com/watch?v=m8rRzTtP7Tc&t=271s.

importantly, just imagine the long term positive impact it will have on children's lives and wellbeing. This is yet another seed that will grow into a society with less violence, less substance abuse, fewer incarcerated individuals, and more empathy.

Chapter 6: Physical Health and Nutrition

"It is easier to build strong children than to repair broken men."

- Frederick Douglass

The health and wellbeing of our nation is at stake. Our current education system does not properly help students learn or practice the three elements that lead to a physically healthy life. The system even prevents it in a few different ways. Most people can guess the first two elements: Fitness and Nutrition. However, the third remains largely a mystery, yet it is just as important as the other two. Do you know what it is? Sleep. Let's take a look at each in turn.

Nutrition

Not everyone knows that two of the top killers in the U.S., heart disease and diabetes, are often caused by diet.[35] In addition most lack the knowledge to practice a healthy diet. Not even all physicians receive nutrition training, yet proper nutrition is preventative medicine. As is stated in a *Journal of Biomedical Education* article, "poor nutrition contributes to the development of most chronic diseases and even some acute conditions. The ongoing obesity epidemic demands urgent attention from physicians."[36] However, "physicians in the U.S. are largely on their

[35] "National Center for Health Statistics." Centers for Disease Control and Prevention. March 17, 2017. Accessed November 13, 2018. https://www.cdc.gov/nchs/fastats/leading-causes-of-death.htm.

[36] Adams, Kelly M., W. Scott Butsch, and Martin Kohlmeier. "The State of Nutrition Education at US Medical Schools." Journal of Biomedical Education 2015 (2015): 1-7. doi:10.1155/2015/357627.

own when it comes to learning how to look for signs of nutrition problems, how to explain the significance of nutrition-related conditions and appropriate interventions, and how to refer patients to nutrition professionals." A Chinese proverb says, "the superior doctor prevents sickness. The mediocre doctor attends to impending sickness. The inferior doctor treats actual sickness." This proverb makes it easy to blame the doctor when you get sick, but we can and should take our health into our own hands. We should teach our children how to care for themselves by understanding proper nutrition.

Movement

In addition to teaching kids about preventative medicine with proper nutrition, we need to make sure their physical needs are met as well. "Sitting disease" is being inactive for more than six hours per day.[37] Doing so greatly increases premature death. A Mayo Clinic study showed that sitting is just as bad as smoking when it comes to heart disease.[38] Another study showed that inactivity kills more people worldwide than does

[37] The term "Sitting Disease" has been coined by the scientific community and is commonly used when referring to metabolic syndrome and the ill-effects of an overly sedentary lifestyle. However, the medical community does not recognize Sitting Disease as a diagnosable disease at this time.

[38] Laskowski, M.D. Edward R. "Sitting Risks: How Harmful Is Too Much Sitting?" Mayo Clinic. May 08, 2018. Accessed August 15, 2018. https://www.mayoclinic.org/healthy-lifestyle/adult-health/expert-answers/sitting/faq-20058005.

smoking.[39] Yet another study found that even if you exercise a lot, perhaps one hour a day, it may still not be enough to counteract the bad effects of extended periods of sitting.[40] If you spend most of your time sitting you are at greater risk of death from any cause. One needs to be moving all day. Yet most of our students spend their days sitting at a desk.

Angela Hanscom, an occupational therapist and founder of Timber Nook, visited a middle school in her local community.[41] Her intention was to sit still and pay attention just as we expect students to do. After what she describes as an excruciating 90 minutes she found that even she could not keep from fidgeting. She knew there was no way she could tolerate this for six hours let alone every day. She explains,

Their bodies aren't designed for extended periods of sitting. In fact, none of our bodies are made to stay sedentary for lengths of time. This lack of movement and unrelenting sitting routine are

[39] Yeager, Selene. "Sitting Is the New Smoking- Even for Runners." Runner's World. May 25, 2018. Accessed August 15, 2018. https://www.runnersworld.com/health-injuries/a20796415/sitting-is-the-new-smoking-even-for-runners/.

[40] "Sitting Disease By The Numbers Infographic." JustStand.org. Accessed August 15, 2018. https://www.juststand.org/resource/infographics/sitting-disease-by-the-numbers/.

[41] Strauss, Valerie. "A Therapist Goes to Middle School and Tries to Sit Still and Focus. She Can't. Neither Can the Kids." The Washington Post. December 03, 2014. Accessed August 15, 2018. https://www.washingtonpost.com/news/answer-sheet/wp/2014/12/03/a-therapist-goes-to-middle-school-and-tries-to-sit-still-and-focus-she-cant-neither-can-the-kids/?noredirect=on&utm_term=.dbcb4a4b8768

*wreaking havoc on their bodies and minds. Bodies start to
succumb to these unnatural positions and sedentary lifestyles
through atrophy of the muscles, tightness of ligaments (where
there shouldn't be tightness), and underdeveloped sensory systems
– setting them up for weak bodies, poor posturing, and inefficient
sensory processing of the world around them.*

But what struck me the most was the fact that the same school converted snack time to a working snack time, recess has been lost due to the fear of children getting injured, and physical education has been reduced to once every sixth day! Occasionally, there is an entire week the children will go with no physical education at all. Why are we doing this to children?

Unfortunately, I have met some who suggest the teachers are clueless about the need for children to move, but that is simply not the case. They are actually quite frustrated with the situation. A number of teachers explained to Angela,

*"We are expected to cram more and more information down their
throats."*

"It is insane! We can no longer teach according to what we feel is

developmentally appropriate."

"Due to the high-stakes testing, even project-based learning opportunities are no longer feasible. Too many regulations, not enough time."

Just imagine the long-term effects this will have on our children. Not only should we prioritize teaching our students about fitness, we also need to keep them moving throughout their days. One of the many ways this could be accomplished is by "flipping" the classroom. The typical structure as of now is lecture in the classroom, and then sending the students home to attempt application alone. However, in a flipped classroom. their homework is a brief video lecture. The next day application happens in the classroom with their peers and guided by the teacher. This gives time for getting the students up and about while in class. They can be collaborative and experiment. There is class time to try kinesthetic ways to learn the lesson. Flipping the classroom is a simple way to make learning more active and practical.

Sleep

The health of our bodies is impacted by more than nutrition and fitness.

Sleep also plays a vital role in our health and wellbeing, and we simply aren't getting enough of it. For 95% of the population, less than seven to nine hours of sleep will result in sleep deprivation.[42] Being sleep deprived is equivalent to being drunk on the road. You are less likely to be satisfied with your job if you are sleep deprived, your immune system is likely to suffer, and sleep deprivation leads to depression, anxiety, and suicide.[43] Studies have also found that children need more sleep than adults and also tend to do better at different times of the day. While young children tend to wake early, the American Academy of Pediatrics (AAP) explains that beginning at puberty, kids' sleep-wake cycles begin to shift up to two hours later.[44] Not only is it hard for them to get up in the morning; it is hard for them to get to sleep before 11:00 at night. A poll by the National Sleep Foundation (NSF) found that 59% of 6th through 8th graders and 87% of high school students in the U.S. were getting less than the recommended

[42] Duval, Sylviane. "Most High School Students Are Sleep Deprived." Doctor-Patient Relationship Influences Patient Engagement | Center for Advancing Health. Accessed August 15, 2018. http://www.cfah.org/hbns/2010/most-high-school-students-are-sleep-deprived.

[43] Rodriguez, Tori. "Teenagers Who Don't Get Enough Sleep at Higher Risk for Mental Health Problems." Scientific American. July 01, 2015. Accessed August 15, 2018. https://www.scientificamerican.com/article/teenagers-who-don-t-get-enough-sleep-at-higher-risk-for-mental-health-problems/.

[44] "Let them sleep" AAP.Org Accessed August 15, 2018. https://www.aap.org/en-us/about-the-aap/aap-press-room/pages/let-them-sleep-aap-recommends-delaying-start-times-of-middle-and-high-schools-to-combat-teen-sleep-deprivation.aspx.

8 1⁄2 to 9 1⁄2 hours of sleep on school nights.[45] As a matter of fact I myself worked with a number of high schools that started their days at 7 AM. I understand that school schedules are a major logistical consideration. However, starting at 7 AM for high school students should simply be unacceptable. If we were to see a baby out and about at 10 or 11 O'clock at night, we would be concerned for the wellbeing of that child. We should have the same concern for waking teenagers early in the morning.

We need to redesign schools to support and aid students in receiving the sleep that they need. What will the logistics of that be? What will it look like? I'm not sure yet but I am sure the topic needs to be on the table.

---

[45] "2006 Teens and Sleep." National Sleep Foundation. Accessed August 15, 2018. https://sleepfoundation.org/sleep-polls-data/sleep-in-america-poll/2006-teens-and-sleep.

Chapter 7: Financial Literacy

"Chains of habit are too light to be felt until they are too heavy to

be broken."

- Warren Buffett

Dave Ramsey explains how teens can become millionaires:

Ben and Arthur were friends who grew up together. They both knew that they needed to start thinking about the future. At age 19, Ben decided to invest $2,000 every year for eight years. He picked investment funds that averaged a 12% interest rate. Then, at age 26, Ben stopped putting money into his investments. So he put a total of $16,000 into his investment funds.

Now, Arthur didn't start investing until age 27. Just like Ben, he put $2,000 into his investment funds every year until he turned 65. He got the same 12% interest rate as Ben, but he invested 23 more years than Ben did. So Arthur invested a total of $78,000 over 39 years.

When both Ben and Arthur turned 65, they decided to compare their investment accounts. Who do you think had more? Ben, with his total of $16,000 invested over eight years, or Arthur, who invested $78,000 over 39 years? Believe it or not, Ben came out ahead ... $700,000 ahead! Arthur had a total of $1,532,166, while Ben had a total of $2,288,996. How did he do *it? Starting early is the key. He put in less money, but started eight years earlier. That's compound interest for you! It turns $16,000 into almost $2.3 million! Since Ben invested earlier, the interest kicked in sooner.*[46]

Like many before and after me, I did not understand compound interest when I was a freshman in college. I barely learned budgeting basics, much less understood investing, and even that was by trial and error. But I at least understood how checking accounts worked. In my first semester I overheard a few interesting conversations from others just learning how to manage their finances. Here are two of the most memorable:

In a panicked voice, "What do you mean it bounced? … But, I just wrote a check. I didn't do anything!"   And on another occasion by a different student I heard in a confident voice, "I'll go to the ATM and if nothing comes out I'll just write you check."

The average credit score for ages 18-24 is 630-643.[47] It is no surprise considering most schools in the U.S. either do not offer personal

---

[46] Ramsey Solutions. "How Teens Can Become Millionaires." Daveramsey.com. May 14, 2018. Accessed August 15, 2018. https://www.daveramsey.com/blog/how-teens-can-become-millionaires.

[47] "Chart of the Week: What Is the Average Credit Score for 18-24 Year Olds?" Next Gen Personal Finance: Home. Accessed August 15, 2018. https://www.ngpf.org/blog/credit-scores/chart-of-the-week-what-is-the-average-credit-score-for-18-24-year-olds/.

finance education at all or it is not prioritized. A math teacher who wanted to teach personal finances was told it was not rigorous enough. In one school I visited they did teach personal finance but it was a remedial math course. At another school I frequented, in an elective business class the teacher snuck in some personal finance.

Yet one of the first things our children will have to consider when they become adults is how to finance their higher education. We do not come close to adequately preparing students for that immense decision. In my time as a college and career coach I discovered that a surprising number of students did not even know the difference between a scholarship and a loan. Some students thought both were free money and yet others thought both were borrowed money. Many even thought tuition included living expenses.

Students are strongly encouraged to attend college after high school, and that is about where the conversation ends. The financial realities of college and degree choice is rarely, if ever, discussed. These days it takes more than just asking "so, where do you want to go and what do you want to major in" to make a sound decision. We need to be helping teenagers to calculate their return on investment for their higher education. We should teach students to consider how much aid they may receive based on their circumstances, the scholarships at the schools they are considering, the tuition costs for their schools and degrees of choice, what amount of debt can they expect upon graduating, and how much income they are likely to make once in their fields.

Knowing and evaluating these things is more important now than ever. Let's take a look at a few facts.

Approximate average cost for 2016-2017 year:[48]

Private tuition - $33,000

Public Out-of-State tuition - $25,000

Public In-State tuition - $10,000

Housing and Meals - $10-11,000

Books and supplies - $1,200

Personal transportation - $2-3,000

[48] "What's the Price Tag for a College Education?" COLLEGEdata. Accessed August 15, 2018. https://www.collegedata.com/cs/content/content_payarticle_tmpl.jhtml?articleId=10064.

Financial aid not including loans - \$2,000-\$12,000[49]

The cost of tuition has drastically increased compared to the increase in wages over the past decades. While in the 1960s and 1970s a person could earn their tuition money with a summer or part-time job, this is no longer the case.[50] It is now a necessity for most students to seek loans. The Institute for College Access & Success tells us that the average student borrower graduates with approximately \$30,000 of debt.[51] This drastic increase in tuition alongside only a slight increase in wages also means that the return on investment has decreased significantly as well. This, combined with rampant predatory lending, has made it nearly impossible for many to come out of the hole they are in when they begin their lives and careers.

It may surprise you that over 40 countries around the world offer free post-secondary education, including: Germany, Denmark, Greece,

---

[49] "Digest of Education Statistics, 2010." Revenues and Expenditures for Public Elementary and Secondary Education: School Year 2001-2002, E.D. Tab. Accessed August 15, 2018. https://nces.ed.gov/programs/digest/d10/tables/dt10_351.asp.

[50] "Median Incomes v. Average College Tuition Rates, 1971-2016 - College Education - ProCon.org." ProConorg Headlines. Accessed August 15, 2018. https://college-education.procon.org/view.resource.php?resourceID=005532.

[51] "Project on Student Debt." The Institute For College Access and Success. Accessed August 15, 2018. https://ticas.org/posd/map-state-data.

Argentina, Kenya, Morocco, Egypt, Uruguay, Scotland, and Turkey. Many countries even offer courses in English allowing international students to benefit from their free tuition. Some of the best places for Americans to do this are: Brazil, Germany, Finland, France, Norway, Slovenia, and Sweden. International students still need to cover living expenses but tuition is free.[52]

When we do not teach our kids financial understanding we set our students up for financial stress. Money is in fact the biggest cause of stress in the United States.[53] Stress, as many of us know, causes many health problems, such as high blood pressure, heart disease, obesity, and diabetes.[54] By not teaching even the basics of personal finance and then expecting kids to go to a college they cannot afford, we are literally setting them up for failure. The effect that this has on their lives and their health could easily be avoided with proper education.

Some argue that they do not want to concern kids with money or

---

[52] "College Access and Affordability: USA vs. the World." Value Colleges. November 01, 2016. Accessed August 15, 2018. https://www.valuecolleges.com/collegecosts/.

[53] Stress in America: The State of Our Nation. Report. American Psychological Association. Apa.org, 2017.

[54] The American Psychological Association tells us that stress is up, children are hurting, self-care isn't a priority, and Americans lack the willpower to adopt healthier behaviors. All of these things could be remedied with a redesign of our education system.
Clay, R.A. "Stressed in America." Monitor on Psychology. January 2011. Accessed August 15, 2018. http://www.apa.org/monitor/2011/01/stressed-america.aspx.

budgets. However, being upfront with children about monthly bills, budgeting, making payments on time, shopping, paychecks, and for the right ages, even investments, loans, and insurance will teach them that money does come from somewhere and it has a purpose greater than buying ourselves fun things. All students deserve to be given the tools to have a positive money mindset and understanding that they can take into adulthood.

It is even more imperative now that we ensure individuals receive financial education. For example, past generations depended on pensions for the bulk of their retirement funds. The financial burden fell on the companies or government funding them. Consumers did not contribute their own funds or have to make decisions. Today, however, pensions are rare. Some employees will be offered the ability to contribute their own funds to a 401k in which they will make investment decisions. Those with no 401k options will need to educate themselves independently to find retirement funding options and make decisions. Also, Social Security, which was a major source of retirement income, may not be available at all in the future. The Social Security Board of Trustees reported that by 2034 the Social Security trust fund may be depleted.[55] Consumers are also faced with far more complex options for any major investment – home, education, car – than in the past. Products offer many more interest rates and maturities than previously.

Chartered financial analyst Kristina Zucchi of Investopedia points out that the lack of financial literacy is not just a U.S. problem.[56] It is a global problem regardless of socioeconomic status, regardless of a country's economic development. More than half of populations in nations across the world do not understand financial basics. In our fast-changing world economy financial ignorance is more dangerous than ever before.[57]

The good news is that there are resources and tools out there that guide us in teaching age appropriate financial lessons to kids. These include Life Hub Learning Center which teaches banking to kids. Some simple tips come from Parents.com.[58] And even Dave Ramsey has a blog post that

---

[55] Kunkel, Sue. "A SUMMARY OF THE 2018 ANNUAL REPORTS." Social Security History. Accessed August 15, 2018. https://www.ssa.gov/oact/trsum/.

[56] Zucchi, CFA Kristina. "Why Financial Literacy Is so Important." Investopedia. March 19, 2018. Accessed August 15, 2018. https://www.investopedia.com/articles/investing/100615/why-financial-literacy-and-education-so-important.asp.

[57] Cussen, Mark P. "Top 5 Reasons Why People Go Bankrupt." Investopedia. March 26, 2010. Accessed August 15, 2018. https://www.investopedia.com/slide-show/top-5-reasons-why-people-go-bankrupt/.

[58] Skolnik, Deborah. "Teaching Kids About Money." Parents. October 06, 2005. Accessed August 15, 2018. https://www.parents.com/toddlers-preschoolers/development/intellectual/teaching-kids-about-money/.

gives you tips on teaching kids about money. This would be an easy adaptation to our schools especially considering this is one of the most tangible ways to teach math. I remember in my high school Trigonometry class asking my teacher why we were learning how to graph curves. She told me that the formulas we were using to graph curves were the process used for contact lens prescriptions. Why? Why do our teenagers need to know that? Of all of The Five Happy Healthy Elements, this one may be the most obvious. Of course we need to teach financial literacy and it has the most straightforward application. There is plenty of rigorous math involved in finances. All we need to do is prioritize it.

Chapter 8: Community Involvement and Effective Altruism

"Everybody can be great ... because everybody can serve."

- MLK

Emotional health and physical health help children learn how to manage their inner world. However, they also need to learn how to relate to their outer world. Financial Literacy is one way in which we relate to our outer world. It is through community involvement and effective altruism that we begin to help children see beyond themselves and their immediate circle. This is where we teach children to become globally and culturally aware individuals connecting to those who are different than us. Let me quickly define the difference between altruism and effective altruism.[59] Altruism is the concern for the wellbeing of others. Effective altruism is when we take action on that concern to make a positive difference in the wellbeing of others. The movement of effective altruism also emphasizes strategic action so that we can have a greater impact.

Living in a democratic and positive society requires effort. It requires an informed, effective, and responsible citizenry. However, at the moment, barely more than half of the population in the U.S. votes in the presidential election and even fewer vote for local officials. Only a quarter of the

---

[59] "Introduction to Effective Altruism." Effective Altruism. Accessed August 15, 2018. https://www.effectivealtruism.org/articles/introduction-to-effective-altruism/.

population volunteers to participate in their communities.[60] By participating in civic duties, individuals learn that their actions affect more than themselves and have an impact on others.

When students are involved in community service, they learn civic duty as well as effective altruism, and their participation benefits them in a number of other ways:

- As students work within their community, they learn that they can be responsible for making great things happen which in turn builds a sense of responsibility and pride.

- Students who participate in community service learning tend to do better in school.

- Students who do community service work learn that they can actually make a difference with what they do.

- Often, students who have participated in community service will grow up to become young voters and remain involved in their communities throughout their lives.

- Community service is a great problem-solving skill builder.

[60] "Volunteering in the United States, 2015." U.S. Bureau of Labor Statistics. February 25, 2016. Accessed August 15, 2018. https://www.bls.gov/news.release/volun.nr0.htm.

- Research has shown that individuals who participate in volunteering have better physical and mental health than those who do not.[61]

- Taking part in community service teaches students skills that are valuable to employers.

- Community service opens students up to a wealth of networking opportunities.

- Participating in community service allows students to build upon their existing skill sets.

- Students will learn to work in teams and perhaps learn leadership skills.

- Students may have the chance to build relationships with individuals from other cultures.

Often it is wondered, can altruism be taught? It can be and it should be. Philosophers, ethologists, and evolutionary biologists all speculate that a species marked more by altruism than by aggression has a better chance to

---

[61] Watson, Stephanie. "Volunteering May Be Good for Body and Mind." Harvard Health Blog. October 30, 2015. Accessed November 05, 2018. https://www.health.harvard.edu/blog/volunteering-may-be-good-for-body-and-mind-201306266428.

survive.[62] A Chinese proverb says, "if you want happiness for a lifetime, help somebody else." In fact only 10% of happiness levels lie in life circumstances. About 40% of our happiness lies in things that are within our control, and kindness is one of them.[63] However, according to a national survey conducted by the Making Caring Common Project, only 20% of youth say that caring for others is a top priority.[64] Youth are three times more likely to agree than disagree with this statement: "my parents are prouder if I get good grades than if I'm a caring community member."

The good news is that increasing kindness is simpler than it might seem. It turns out altruism comes naturally to kids. According to Psychologist Michael Tomasello, they begin showing altruistic tendencies as early as two years old.[65] While many people know this stage as the "terrible twos" it is also the "little helper" stage. They have an almost reflexive desire to help. As they grow they begin to learn what it means to

---

[62] Raz, Guy. "Wired For Altruism." NPR. Accessed August 15, 2018. https://www.npr.org/programs/ted-radio-hour/529942441/wired-for-altruism.

[63] Lyubomirsky, Sonja, Ph.D. "What Influences Our Happiness the Most?" Psychology Today (blog), May 4, 2008. Accessed December 6, 2018. https://www.psychologytoday.com/us/blog/how-happiness/200805/what-influences-our-happiness-the-most.

[64] "Making Caring Common." Making Caring Common. Accessed August 15, 2018. https://mcc.gse.harvard.edu/.

[65] Tomasello is co-director of the Max Planck Institute for Evolutionary Anthropology in Leipzig, Germany

be part of a group. Their cooperation is affected by their surroundings and what others think of them. Tomassello states, "they arrive at the process with a predisposition for helpfulness and cooperation. But then they learn to be selective about whom to help, inform and share with, and they also learn to manage the impression they are making on others—their public reputation and self — as a way of influencing the actions of those others toward themselves."[66] All we as educators and parents need to do is continue to encourage the altruistic behavior as they grow.

As with anything, if you want something to become a habit you need to be a part of a community that already lives that habit. When children live in a reality in which community involvement is par for the course they will be more likely to carry the habit into adulthood. Our schools can create an environment where altruism, civic duty, and multicultural awareness are a regular part of students' lives.

A great example came from an interview I did with Becky Morales, teacher and founder of Kid World Citizen, as we were talking about

---

[66] Gorlick, Adam. "For Kids, Altruism Comes Naturally, Psychologist Says." Stanford University. November 05, 2008. Accessed August 15, 2018. https://news.stanford.edu/news/2008/november5/tanner-110508.html.

global education.[67] She told me a story,

> One example was a day when we had kids bring their families to talk to the class. One of the grandparents mentioned that their family lives in a nursing home. She mentioned that a lot of the people who live in the nursing home were sad because not a lot of people come to visit them. The kids asked the teacher if they could make cards for the people in the nursing home. The kids saw a need and took action. They decided to make cards during their Valentine's Day party and some kids got to go deliver them. They are thinking outside of their immediate group, they considered another perspective, and then they took action. It's about how we are all connected. The ideas for activities are student led, it's finding something they are passionate about.[68]

Luckily with a quick Google search parents can find ideas for their families to start participating in service at any age. And schools have already acknowledged the importance of service learning. Service learning programs began in some schools in the 1970s. However, in my experience

[67] Morales, Becky. "Activities That Help Young Minds Go Global." Kid World Citizen. Accessed August 15, 2018. https://kidworldcitizen.org/.

[68] Morales, Becky. Telephone interview by author. June 9, 2017.

as a student and as a professional I have not seen it made a priority yet. Service learning could be made a focal point, as well as being incorporated into subjects by using service projects as a practical and active way to teach a lesson for the subject. Here are some ideas:

- Biology - service project to help animals in need.

- Culinary arts - service project about reducing food waste by feeding the hungry.

- Literacy - taking little ones to story time at an assisted living facility.

- Arts programs - creating or performing art for hospitals.

- Math - planning a fundraiser, or seeking out sponsors for a charity.

I could go on, but instead I am going to challenge you to find more ideas.

Chapter 9: Learning Through Interests Rather Than Subjects

"Every day our children spread their dreams beneath our feet. We should tread softly."

- Sir Ken Robinson

Alex, a D.C. student participating in a project sponsored by the Challenger Center for Space Science Education, was working on how to cook his favorite food – hamburgers – in space.[69] Marsville, a colony he designed on the fourth planet from the sun, wouldn't be complete without burgers. In order to solve this problem he began consulting with a British scientist. The scientist told Alex he would soon be visiting D.C. for a National Science meeting and suggested they "do lunch." As Alex told his teacher this, he began to cry. When she asked why he was crying he explained that he had not told the scientist that he was only in the fourth grade and that he didn't know "how to do lunch." I love this story because it illustrates just how far kids can go when they are given the time and guidance to explore what interests them. This story took place in the 1990s. Unfortunately, schools have changed drastically since then and at many schools around the country there is less and less freedom for the teachers to allow this kind of in-depth exploration.

When the structure of our school system was initially designed, separating the subjects was a tool used to prevent true conceptual

---

[69] Sutton, Bonnie Bracey. "The Teacher as a Guide: Letting Students Navigate Their Own Learning." Edutopia. Accessed August 15, 2018. https://www.edutopia.org/teacher-learning-guide.

learning. This was done to stay in line with the original intent of preventing independent thinking and creating a compliant citizenry, but independent thinking is exactly what today's economy needs. Employers want innovative, creative staff. However, because school has been structured this way since the 18th century, it can be difficult to imagine doing it any other way. Other methods of teaching have been proven effective and were attempted in the past. In the end, they were not implemented at the time because they were too costly to scale. However, with current technology, this is no longer a problem. We now have the technologies and tools that we need to provide a better way of learning. As the needs of economies and industries have changed through the generations, it has also become imperative that we do find a new way to convey information in the educational arena.

Finland, which leads the world in education, just recently announced that they will begin exploring an interest-focused structure for their older students.[70] Instead of subjects, students will study *topics* or *phenomena* in an interdisciplinary format. For example, the study of World War II will

---

[70] Zareva, Teodora. "The Latest School Reform in Finland Introduces a New Way to Look at Subjects." Big Think. November 14, 2016. Accessed August 15, 2018. https://bigthink.com/design-for-good/the-latest-school-reform-in-finland-introduces-a-new-way-to-look-at-subjects.

include history, geography, and math. After completing a course called "Working in a Cafe" students will have a body of knowledge having to do with language, economics, and communication.

I have heard concern that if we eliminate subjects to focus on interests, there will be gaps in kids' learning. Of course children will receive the literacy and numeracy foundation they need, but it will be done through exploration of interests. In other words, classical "subjects" such as Math, Reading, Science, etc. are not eliminated entirely but are byproducts of this kind of education. For example, exploring deeply into the interest of food will include many subjects from Health and Nutrition, to Math, Biology, Chemistry, Geology, Botany, and Anthropology. It is kinesthetic and aesthetic. In addition to science, artistic elements are involved; flavor, texture, balance, color, etc. This is one of my favorite examples, not only because I love food, but also because the Culinary Arts are an area of interest that ignites all of the senses.

Shifting to an interest-based method will also allow the role of teachers to shift. When schools were initially created, they were one of the very rare places where a person could get information. When books were rare and incredibly expensive, lecture was the best format to receive the information. But, as you know, information is abundant and accessible in the 21st century. The question now becomes how do we evaluate the information we find? With interest-based learning, students will engage in a way that leads to self-directed learning. The teacher's role can now shift to being a guide. He can help the students plan their process and set goals. She can be collaborative with her students, observe, assist, and suggest. This is one of the keys to creating a more individualized learning process.

This shift is being seen in a few schools here in the States as well. A school in rural New Hampshire began a "student-centered learning" program in 2012.[71] Student-led discussions, small-group work, and individual projects dominate. Rather than the traditional grading system, they use a matrix of "competencies," detailing the skills and knowledge that students are expected to master in each class. Teachers review how closely their instruction is aligning with the competencies. Using an online database, they are able to continually track individual student growth. Students can also take additional online classes to further challenge

---

[71] Richmond, Emily. "When Students Take Over the Classroom." The Atlantic. October 24, 2014. Accessed August 15, 2018. https://www.theatlantic.com/education/archive/2014/10/what-happens-when-students-control-their-own-education/381828/.

themselves or even earn college credit. Family engagement is a key part of each student's progress. And the Extended Learning Opportunities (ELO) program allows students to earn credit for workplace experiences that reinforce their academic studies, such as interning at a dentist's office or the local radio station.

Another amazing example of student led learning comes from a school in California that no longer separates children by age.[72] Grouping kids by age is arbitrary and has nothing to do with how children learn or develop. Mixing age groups provides an entire method of learning that isn't happening in most schools today – peer-to-peer mentorship. One of the best ways to learn something is to teach it, and that is exactly what the Oakland School is implementing. Older students are mentoring, tutoring, and leading. It works well; these multi-aged groups are out-performing the standard structure in every area.

Of course, students need and will receive the fundamentals. But redesigning and restructuring our schools to allow for learning through deep exploration of interests will do more than just teach literacy and

[72] "Urban Montessori Charter School." Urban Montessori Charter School. Accessed August 15, 2018. http://www.urbanmontessori.org/.

numeracy. It fosters curiosity, allows for mastery, it teaches how to learn, instills confidence, allows us to take responsibility for our learning, allows us to know ourselves well, set goals for ourselves, and creates a mindset that will lead to lifelong learning. In addition to the Five Happy Healthy Elements, this type of learning will create employability skills and life skills that are needed to navigate a global society and live a life of happiness and fulfillment.

Chapter 10: Transforming Education for a Thriving Generation

"We do not need magic to transform our world. We carry all the power we need inside ourselves already."

- JK Rowling

The journey that led to this book was not only sparked by the question "what's the point of school," but also the question "what is happening to our kids?" We've seen a drastic increase in depression, anxiety, suicide, and violence. I searched for and found a number of things that cause these outcomes: sleep deprivation, lack of free play, lack of physical movement, poor nutritional health, negative relationships, stress, and lack of stress management techniques.

While I was already aware that our education system does not teach students to cope with or manage these things, I was saddened to learn that the way our schools are designed, structured, and prioritized seems to be contributing to them. Let's review what we learned in previous chapters:

- Sleep deprivation - 59% of 6-8th graders and 87% of high schoolers are sleep deprived. As children age their internal clocks shift later, yet school schedules require students to start their days early.

- Lack of free play - Recess is being lost due to fear of injury, and children have hours of homework.

- Lack of physical movement - Physical education is being reduced. Increased testing leads to less class time for kinesthetic learning.

- Poor nutritional health - Nutrition education is only offered as an elective at some schools.

- Negative relationships - Teaching kids what to do about negative interactions is rarely taught in general.

- Stress - Kids are being tested as young as six years old. The overemphasis on grades, tests, and college admittance causes a large amount of stress. Also, lack of financial literacy education leads to money stress later in life.

- Lack of stress management techniques - It is rare to see this kind of education anywhere.

It may be that our schools are a significant contributor to these increases in mental disorders and violence. Our kids deserve better. Our kids' futures need better. And it is time that we halt and redirect our education system.

If anything else harmed our kids in this way we would be in the streets demanding better. So why aren't we? Many are still unaware of just how dire the situation is, but that can change by making this a national conversation. Some *are* trying to take action. Teachers are on the front lines, working to make it better for kids now in spite of the system. Unfortunately, as the goal and structure remains the same, teachers' hard work at best neutralizes the situation. Some parents *have* taken action by home/unschooling their kids or finding alternative schools. But what about kids whose parent can't choose those options? What about kids who don't have a parent willing to advocate for them? What about kids who don't have a parent? That is why we need to grow this movement. Why we, as a society, need to take action to influence a transformation of the system.

The Strategy

For a transformation to take place like the one I envision, a few things need to happen. First, it requires a cultural shift, a grassroots movement. A grassroots movement isn't organized by political forces. It isn't something that starts with a decision maker way up the ladder. It begins with communities and it spreads. The movement changes the culture which then makes it impossible for the system not to change. If we can can think, view, and talk about education in a new way, then we can influence a change of the system. Once this culture shift has taken hold the next step is to change the goal of our system. Once the goal has changed to helping kids live thriving, fulfilling lives by teaching them happy healthy habits then we will be able to start the redesign process.

So, how does this translate to our daily lives? What can we do on a regular basis to help usher in this culture shift? That depends on who you are. Below I have listed some ideas.

Students

First, I want to tell you to breathe. Breathe and let the stress go. It's not easy to do when you have been immersed in it for so long, but I encourage you to take the initiative to learn how.

Next, I want you to keep in mind that while many of the people who go to the "best" colleges end up successful, there are many who are not successful despite going to the "best" colleges. And there many who are wonderfully successful despite being educated at lesser-known schools. I once had a teacher tell me that it wasn't about where I went to school, it was what I put into it. I resented her for that. I thought she told me that because deep down she knew I couldn't hack it. I thought she was trying to get me to give up on my dream school. Now I realize she didn't mean it that way at all. In fact, she meant the opposite. She knew I would accomplish what I wanted no matter where I went. That is true for you, as well. If you really want to accomplish something, you will. So, try for that dream school. Why not? Don't go for the school someone else is trying to convince you of. And if you don't end up where you were hoping, don't let it stop you. You can still accomplish what you want regardless of what kind of school or kind of further education you have.

Take the time to discover who you are and what you want for your life. It may feel like you have to wait until you're out of high school, until you're an adult, to take control of your own lives and education, but you don't have to. If you feel you need permission, I hereby give you permission to take your life and your education into your own hands! Find the teachers who are on your side and work with them to make your values a priority. Start clubs or communities that practice the Five Happy Healthy Elements. Organize events. Or just get together with friends to study the things that are of value to you whether that be the 5HHE or whatever interests you.

And finally, for career and life design exploration, I want you to do two things. Visit coursera.org, or download the app, and take the free course *A Life of Happiness and Fulfillment.* Don't worry, you don't have to do the assignments if you don't want to. You can listen to the short, entertaining videos just like you would a podcast. Next, visit liveyourlegend.net. *Live your Legend* has amazing tools for career and self exploration. Also, the community there is a great place to network. Finally, remember that you aren't making a decision, at 18, about how you are going to spend the rest and most of your life. You are just deciding about the next couple of years. If your goals change, that doesn't mean you failed. All it means is that you get to do multiple things in your life.

You've got this!

Parents

Previously I told you about a school in rural New Hampshire doing some exciting new things with a student-centered learning program. It was thanks to the community and parents working with the school's administrators that this change came to fruition. The district was looking for ways to improve local schools and they found overwhelming support from parents for more personalized approaches. Public-private partnerships and the creation of a community working group came up with a new instructional approach. After research, planning, and conversations with parents, the district opted for the student-centered learning model, and the plan was implemented.

Leadership at individual schools still has some power to make refreshing changes that can improve their students' lives. I've even started to hear about schools opting for later start times with great success. Parent groups like PTA or even a self-organized group can start working to influence changes at their children's school. Find kids yoga and mindfulness teachers that offer programs for children and encourage your school to hire them. Push for financial education in math class or in an after school program. Ask your teachers to try a flipped classroom for a few weeks to see how it works out. Ask your school what they are doing to incorporate Social Emotional Learning and/or Service Learning and what you or your parent group can do to ensure they happen. If you utilize an after school program you can make the same suggestions. After school and summer child care programs have more freedom in their curricula. Suggest that they use the 5HHE as a framework for their curriculum design. In the summers or on the weekends, find enrichment programs that are in line with the Five Happy Healthy Elements. You could even start your own groups with other families and allow your kids to create their own Happy Healthy Elements lessons.

Teachers and Child Care Professionals

You are already doing so much for our children with precious little compensation, and we thank you so much for that. In order to make this transformation easier for teachers and not a burden, I am in the process of building a nonprofit resource organization. This nonprofit, Happy Healthy Academy (HHA), has several goals to help teachers, parents, child-care programs, and even students begin to utilize the Five Happy Healthy Elements. HHA maintains a collection of resources that allow educators to easily integrate these elements into their current curriculum or that can be used by parents at home. These resources consist of lessons, materials, programs, websites, books, movies, podcasts, documentaries, etc. Our next goal is to develop Happy Healthy Elements curriculum, free to use, that will also hit the required standards. Next, we will bring services to communities across the country. These services will include field trip options, enrichment classes, summer programs, personalized curriculum development, and community groups. We hope to combine this work with ongoing research to eventually build a brick and mortar school that can serve as a model to influence policy makers.

Community Members

For those who don't currently have children in school but who see the value in transforming our education system now, there are things you can do as well. I encourage you to offer your professional knowledge and skills to local schools, child care programs, homeschool groups, and enrichment camps. This may be on a volunteer basis, but it doesn't have to be. That's up to you. Be willing to take on job shadowers or interns. Open yourself to the possibility of mentoring. The opportunities community members provide are enormously valuable to a young person's experience.

Everyone

Education transformation and this happy healthy goal for our education system need to become part of our nation's dialogue. To join in the conversation and help it grow, follow the hashtags #hhchallenge and #edtransformationnation. Every so often a Happy Healthy Challenge will be issued to the Ed Transformation Nation. You can join the Ed Transformation Nation on Facebook, through email subscription, and/or following on Twitter. We will challenge you to do specific yet simple happy healthy actions with your own families, classrooms, or communities. We'll issue one Happy Healthy Challenge per week, each week focusing on a different Happy Healthy Element. Share your participation in the challenge with a photo or video and the hashtags on any social media platform. Becoming part of the Ed Transformation Nation and participating in the Happy Healthy Challenges are simple and fun ways to start enriching your lives now and grow the transformation conversation.

An Invitation

What *is* the point of school? Right now it is to standardize students. This is accomplished by treating schools as though they are a business. Because schools are treated as a business, they are designed as a factory. Can you guess what the product is? That's right, our kids. And if students are products, that makes colleges the customers. So, it's no wonder testing – regular QA checks – and college admittance are so important to our education system. But this clearly is not working for us, nor do our children deserve to be treated this way. However, we can change this. I invite you to join me in this endeavor. Let us finally prioritize the wellbeing of students. Let us teach kids how to live their best lives for the sake of everyone's futures on this planet. Let us, the Ed Transformation Nation, influence a redesign of our education system from the Industrial structure that it currently has to one that serves students by giving them the gift of thriving, fulfilling lives.

"Some people want it to happen, some people wish it would

happen, others make it happen."

- Michael Jordan

References

"2006 Teens and Sleep." National Sleep Foundation. Accessed August 15, 2018. https://sleepfoundation.org/sleep-polls-data/sleep-in-america-poll/2006-teens-and-sleep.

"About Khan Academy." Khan Academy. Accessed August 15, 2018. https://www.khanacademy.org/about.

Adams, Kelly M., W. Scott Butsch, and Martin Kohlmeier. "The State of Nutrition Education at US Medical Schools." *Journal of Biomedical Education* 2015 (2015): 1-7. doi:10.1155/2015/357627.

"Career and Life Planning in Schools: Multiple Paths; Multiple Policies; Multiple Challenges." People for Education. Accessed August 15, 2018. https://peopleforeducation.ca/report/career-and-life-planning-in-schools-multiple-paths-multiple-policies-multiple-challenges/.

"Chart of the Week: What Is the Average Credit Score for 18-24 Year Olds?" Next Gen Personal Finance: Home. Accessed August 15, 2018. https://www.ngpf.org/blog/credit-scores/chart-of-the-week-what-is-the-average-credit-score-for-18-24-year-olds/.

Clay, R.A. "Stressed in America." Monitor on Psychology. January 2011. Accessed August 15, 2018. http://www.apa.org/monitor/2011/01/stressed-america.aspx.

"College Access and Affordability: USA vs. the World." Value Colleges. November 01, 2016. Accessed August 15, 2018. https://www.valuecolleges.com/collegecosts/.

Cussen, Mark P. "Top 5 Reasons Why People Go Bankrupt." Investopedia. March 26, 2010. Accessed August 15, 2018. https://www.investopedia.com/slide-show/top-5-reasons-why-people-go-bankrupt/.

Diener, Ed. "Pursuit of Happiness." Pursuit of Happiness. Accessed August 15, 2018. http://www.pursuit-of-happiness.org/history-of-happiness/ed-diener/.

"Digest of Education Statistics, 2010." Revenues and Expenditures for Public Elementary and Secondary Education: School Year 2001-2002, E.D. Tab. Accessed August 15, 2018. https://nces.ed.gov/programs/digest/d10/tables/

dt10_351.asp.

"The Digital Industrial Revolution." Interview by Guy Raz. *Https://www.npr.org/programs/ted-radio-hour/522858434/the-digital-industrial-revolution*. Ted Radio Hour. April 21, 2017.

Duckworth, Angela. "Success." Interview. *Https://www.npr.org/2013/10/25/240777690/success*. Ted Radio Hour. November 1, 2013.

Duval, Sylviane. "Most High School Students Are Sleep Deprived." Doctor-Patient Relationship Influences Patient Engagement | Center for Advancing Health. Accessed August 15, 2018. http://www.cfah.org/hbns/2010/most-high-school-students-are-sleep-deprived.

Edutopia. "Pride Advisory Classes: Social and Emotional Support for Every Student." YouTube. March 18, 2016. Accessed August 15, 2018. https://www.youtube.com/watch?v=6BACoWFiRzE.

"EMPOWERING COMMUNITIES." Holistic Me After School Program | Holistic Life Foundation. Accessed August 15, 2018. https://hlfinc.org/.

Fredrickson, Barbara. *Love 2.0: How Our Supreme Emotion Affects Everything We Think, Do, Feel, and Become*. New York: Hudson Street Press, 2013.

"Freelancers Predicted to Become the U.S. Workforce Majority within a Decade, with Nearly 50% of Millennial Workers Already Freelancing, Annual "Freelancing in America" Study Finds | Press, News & Media Coverage." Hiring | Upwork. October 28, 2017. Accessed August 15, 2018. https://www.upwork.com/press/2017/10/17/freelancing-in-america-2017/.

Gorlick, Adam. "For Kids, Altruism Comes Naturally, Psychologist Says." Stanford University. November 05, 2008. Accessed August 15, 2018. https://news.stanford.edu/news/2008/november5/tanner-110508.html.

Gray, Peter, Dr. "The Decline of Play." YouTube. June 13, 2014. Accessed August 15, 2018. https://www.youtube.com/watch?v=Bg-GEzM7iTk.

Grossnationalhappiness.com. Accessed August 15, 2018. http://www.grossnationalhappiness.com/.

"Home - Association of Waldorf Schools of North America." Waldorf Education - Association of Waldorf Schools of North America. Accessed December 12, 2018. https://www.waldorfeducation.org/.

"Introduction to Effective Altruism." Effective Altruism. Accessed August 15, 2018. https://www.effectivealtruism.org/articles/introduction-to-effective-altruism/.

Khan, Salman. *The One World Schoolhouse: Education Reimagined.* New York: Twelve, 2013.

Kunkel, Sue. "A SUMMARY OF THE 2018 ANNUAL REPORTS." Social Security History. Accessed August 15, 2018. https://www.ssa.gov/oact/trsum/.

Laskowski, M.D. Edward R. "Sitting Risks: How Harmful Is Too Much Sitting?" Mayo Clinic. May 08, 2018. Accessed August 15, 2018. https://www.mayoclinic.org/healthy-lifestyle/adult-health/expert-answers/sitting/faq-20058005.

Lazar, Sara. "How Meditation Can Reshape Our Brains." YouTube. January 23, 2012. Accessed August 15, 2018. https://www.youtube.com/watch?v=m8rRzTtP7Tc&t=271s.

"Let-them-sleep-aap-recommends-delaying-start-times-of-middle-and-high-schools-to-combat-teen-sleep-deprivation." Site Title. Accessed August 15, 2018. https://www.aap.org/en-us/about-the-aap/aap-press-room/pages/let-them-sleep-aap-recommends-delaying-start-times-of-middle-and-high-schools-to-combat-teen-sleep-deprivation.aspx.

Levine, Madeline. *Teach Your Children Well: Parenting for Authentic Success.* New York: Harper Perennial, 2013.

Lyubomirsky, Sonja, Ph.D. "What Influences Our Happiness the Most?" *Psychology Today* (blog), May 4, 2008. Accessed December 6, 2018. https://www.psychologytoday.com/us/blog/how-happiness/200805/what-influences-our-happiness-the-most.

"Making Caring Common." Making Caring Common. Accessed August 15, 2018. https://mcc.gse.harvard.edu/.

Marchant, Jo. "Future - Can Meditation Help Prevent the Effects of Ageing?" BBC

News. July 01, 2014. Accessed August 15, 2018. http://www.bbc.com/future/story/20140701-can-meditation-delay-ageing.

McGonigal, Jane. "The Game That Can Give You 10 Extra Years of Life." TED: Ideas worth Spreading. Accessed August 15, 2018. https://www.ted.com/talks/jane_mcgonigal_the_game_that_can_give_you_10_extra_years_of_life.

"Median Incomes v. Average College Tuition Rates, 1971-2016 - College Education - ProCon.org." ProConorg Headlines. Accessed August 15, 2018. https://college-education.procon.org/view.resource.php?resourceID=005532.

Midlarsky, Elizabeth. "What Is Altruism, and Why Is It Important?" Teachers College - Columbia University. December 15, 2011. Accessed August 15, 2018. https://www.tc.columbia.edu/articles/2011/december/what-is-altruism-and-why-is-it-important/.

Morales, Becky. "Activities That Help Young Minds Go Global." Kid World Citizen. Accessed August 15, 2018. https://kidworldcitizen.org/.

"Most New Jobs : Occupational Outlook Handbook:." U.S. Bureau of Labor Statistics. April 13, 2018. Accessed August 15, 2018. https://www.bls.gov/ooh/most-new-jobs.htm.

Perez, Emma B. "What's the Point of School Survey." Whatsthepointsurvey.weebly.com. March 2016. Accessed August 14, 2018. https://whatsthepointsurvey.weebly.com.

"Project on Student Debt." The Institute For College Access and Success. Accessed August 15, 2018. https://ticas.org/posd/map-state-data.

Raghunathan, Rajagopal, Dr. "A Life of Happiness and Fulfillment." Coursera. Accessed August 15, 2018. https://www.coursera.org/learn/happiness.

Ramsey Solutions. "How Teens Can Become Millionaires." Daveramsey.com. May 14, 2018. Accessed August 15, 2018. https://www.daveramsey.com/blog/how-teens-can-become-millionaires.

Raz, Guy. "The Digital Industrial Revolution." NPR. Accessed August 15, 2018. https://www.npr.org/programs/ted-radio-hour/522858434/the-digital-industrial-revolution.

Raz, Guy. "Wired For Altruism." NPR. Accessed August 15, 2018. https://www.npr.org/programs/ted-radio-hour/529942441/wired-for-altruism.

Richmond, Emily. "When Students Take Over the Classroom." The Atlantic. October 24, 2014. Accessed August 15, 2018. https://www.theatlantic.com/education/archive/2014/10/what-happens-when-students-control-their-own-education/381828/.

Robinson, Ken, and Lou Aronica. Creative Schools. UK: Penguin Books, 2016.

Robinson, Ken, Sir. "Do Schools Kill Creativity? | Sir Ken Robinson." YouTube. January 06, 2007. Accessed August 15, 2018. https://www.youtube.com/watch?v=iG9CE55wbtY.

Rodriguez, Tori. "Teenagers Who Don't Get Enough Sleep at Higher Risk for Mental Health Problems." Scientific American. July 01, 2015. Accessed August 15, 2018. https://www.scientificamerican.com/article/teenagers-who-don-t-get-enough-sleep-at-higher-risk-for-mental-health-problems/.

"Sitting Disease By The Numbers Infographic." JustStand.org. Accessed August 15, 2018. https://www.juststand.org/resource/infographics/sitting-disease-by-the-numbers/.

Skolnik, Deborah. "Teaching Kids About Money." Parents. October 06, 2005. Accessed August 15, 2018. https://www.parents.com/toddlers-preschoolers/development/intellectual/teaching-kids-about-money/.

Strauss, Valerie. "A Therapist Goes to Middle School and Tries to Sit Still and Focus. She Can't. Neither Can the Kids." The Washington Post. December 03, 2014. Accessed August 15, 2018. https://www.washingtonpost.com/news/answer-sheet/wp/2014/12/03/a-therapist-goes-to-middle-school-and-tries-to-sit-still-and-focus-she-cant-neither-can-the-kids/?noredirect=on&utm_term=.dbcb4a4b8768.

Stress in America: The State of Our Nation. Report. American Psychological Association. Apa.org, 2017.

Sutton, Bonnie Bracey. "The Teacher as a Guide: Letting Students Navigate Their Own Learning." Edutopia. Accessed August 15, 2018. https://www.edutopia.org/teacher-learning-guide.

Tangney, June P., Roy F. Baumeister, and Angie Luzio Boone. "High Self-Control Predicts Good Adjustment, Less Pathology, Better Grades, and Interpersonal Success." *Journal of Personality* 72, no. 2 (2004): 271-324. doi:10.1111/j. 0022-3506.2004.00263.x.

"The NCES Fast Facts Tool Provides Quick Answers to Many Education Questions (National Center for Education Statistics)." Revenues and Expenditures for Public Elementary and Secondary Education: School Year 2001-2002, E.D. Tab. Accessed August 15, 2018. https://nces.ed.gov/fastfacts/display.asp?id=40.

"Urban Montessori Charter School." Urban Montessori Charter School. Accessed August 15, 2018. http://www.urbanmontessori.org/.

Valet, Vicky. "10 High-Paying Blue-Collar Jobs 2018." Forbes. June 25, 2018. Accessed August 15, 2018. https://www.forbes.com/sites/vickyvalet/ 2018/06/25/10-high-paying-blue-collar-jobs-2018/#2f4778403311.

"Volunteering in the United States, 2015." U.S. Bureau of Labor Statistics. February 25, 2016. Accessed August 15, 2018. https://www.bls.gov/ news.release/volun.nr0.htm.

Walsh, Roger, Dr. 8 Ways to Wellbeing. Accessed August 15, 2018. https://www. 8waystowellbeing.com/.

"What's the Price Tag for a College Education?" COLLEGEdata. Accessed August 15, 2018. https://www.collegedata.com/cs/content/ content_payarticle_tmpl.jhtml?articleId=10064.

Watson, Stephanie. "Volunteering May Be Good for Body and Mind." Harvard Health Blog. October 30, 2015. Accessed November 05, 2018. https:// www.health.harvard.edu/blog/volunteering-may-be-good-for-body-and- mind-201306266428.

WorldEconomicForum. "Jack Ma: "If We Do Not Change the Way We Teach, Thirty Years from Now We Will Be in Trouble."" YouTube. January 24, 2018. Accessed August 15, 2018. https://www.youtube.com/watch?v=pQCF3PtAaSg.

Yeager, Selene. "Sitting Is the New Smoking- Even for Runners." Runner's World. May 25, 2018. Accessed August 15, 2018. https://www.runnersworld.com/ health-injuries/a20796415/sitting-is-the-new-smoking-even-for-runners/.

Zareva, Teodora. "The Latest School Reform in Finland Introduces a New Way to Look at Subjects." Big Think. November 14, 2016. Accessed August 15, 2018. https://bigthink.com/design-for-good/the-latest-school-reform-in-finland-introduces-a-new-way-to-look-at-subjects.

Zucchi, CFA Kristina. "Why Financial Literacy Is so Important." Investopedia. March 19, 2018. Accessed August 15, 2018. https://www.investopedia.com/articles/investing/100615/why-financial-literacy-and-education-so-important.asp.

49047218R00069

Made in the USA
Columbia, SC
18 January 2019